Designed by Flowerpot Press
www.FlowerpotPress.com
CHC-0909-0449
ISBN: 978-1-4867-1486-5
Made in China/Fabriqué en Chine

HOW DO SEESAWS GO UP AND DOWN?

A BOOK ABOUT SIMPLE MACHINES

written by jennifer shand

illustrated by srimalie bassani

WHEEL AND AXLE

WEDGE

LEVER

WHEEL

WHEEL

BICYCLE

AXLE

AXLE

WHEELBARROW

WHEEL & AXLE

FAN

wedge

knife

SCREW

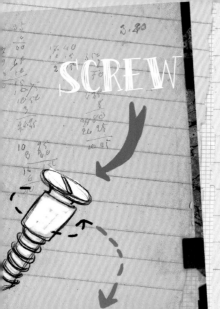

INCLINED PLANE

PULLEY

3 TON

JAR LID

Simple machines are almost everywhere!

Simple machines are really simple, but they are also really helpful! Simple machines can make us seem stronger or faster or both. They are like having superpowers! People have been using simple machines for a long time, and we often put a bunch of simple machines together to make more complicated machines. These are called compound machines. Simple machines are not only important—they can be fun, too!

resistance

inclined plane

force

pulley

CORKSCREW

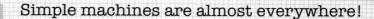

How do you make a seesaw go up and down?
Do you and your friends take turns holding balloons so you float?

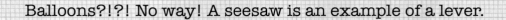
Balloons?!?! No way! A seesaw is an example of a lever.

A lever is usually a stiff board or pole resting across a pivot point. When you push down on the high side of a seesaw the low side rises up. The heavier the person on the low side, the harder you have to push down. They can make it easier by moving closer to the middle or by pushing up. You can make it easier by moving farther away from the middle or by adding a friend.

Why can you almost always ride faster
on a bigger bike than on a smaller bike?
Is it because bigger bikes
have secret rocket boosters?

Rocket boosters?!?! No way! A bicycle is an example of a wheel and axle.

WHEEL AND AXLE

input $\uparrow F_e$

output F_r

wheel

axle

input

output

screwdriver

R $\nearrow F_e$

r

F_r $IMA = \dfrac{R}{r}$

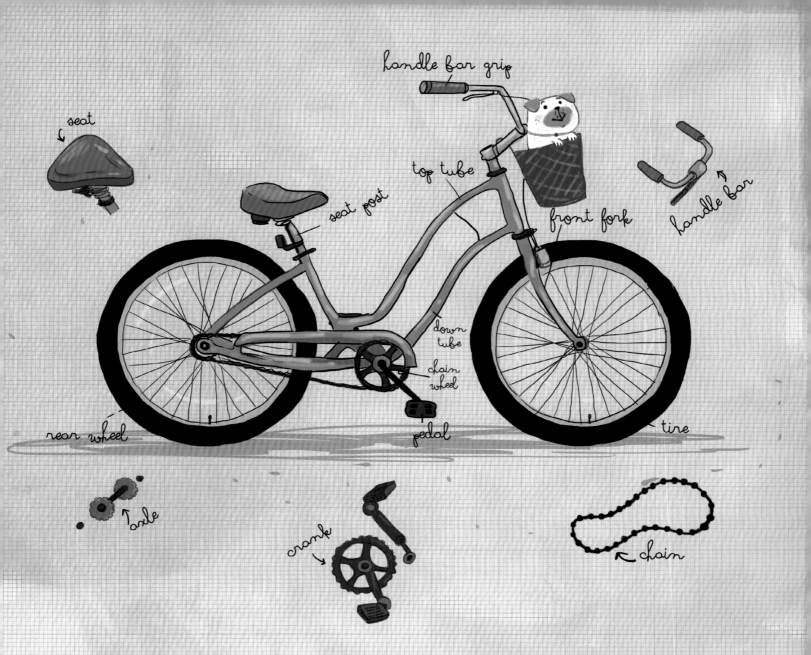

On a bicycle, the wheel is the circle on the outside that spins. The axle is the part in the middle that makes the wheel spin. When you pedal a bike the pedaling makes the axle turn. Every time the axle turns once around, the wheel moves once around. With a BIG wheel you get a BIG tire turn. With a SMALL wheel you get a SMALL tire turn. The bigger the wheel, the bigger the turn, and the faster you go.

How do you raise a flag up a flagpole?
Do you play music to a snake that slides up to the top with the flag?

A snake?!?! No way! Flagpoles use a simple machine called a fixed pulley!

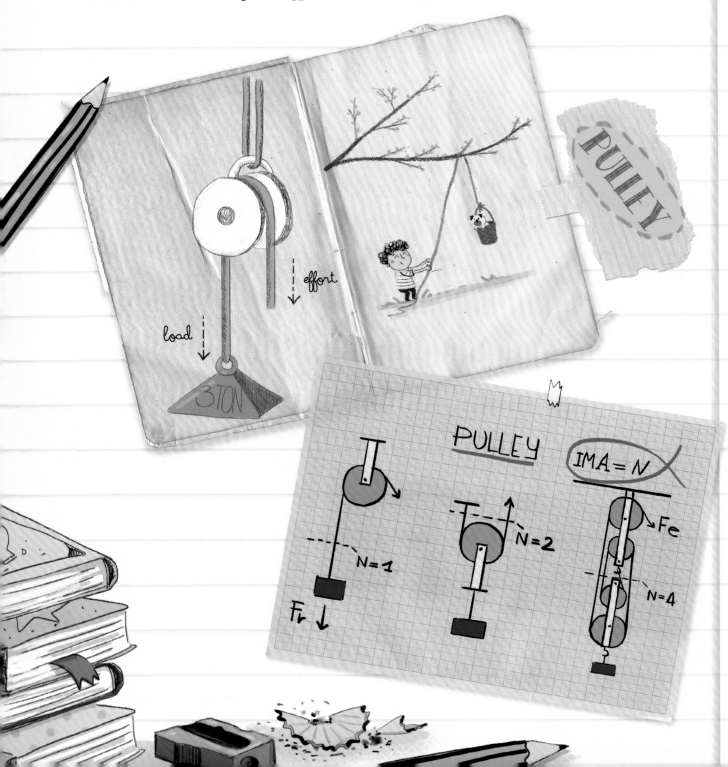

fixed pulley

load

effort

A pulley can change the direction of a force so that you can pull one way and make something move the other way. On a flagpole there is a grooved wheel fixed to the top of a pole and a rope that goes all the way up and then back down again.

When you attach the flag to one side of the rope and pull down on the other side, the flag goes up.

How do cars climb mountains?
Do they have awesome rock climbing skills?

Rock climbing?!?! No way! Cars climb mountains using an inclined plane.

Most cars could not climb a road that goes straight up a mountain. By angling a road up just a little and then winding it back and forth so the climb is spread over a longer distance, the climb becomes much easier.

How does a screw make its way into wood?
Does it dress up really fancy and sneak in the VIP entrance?

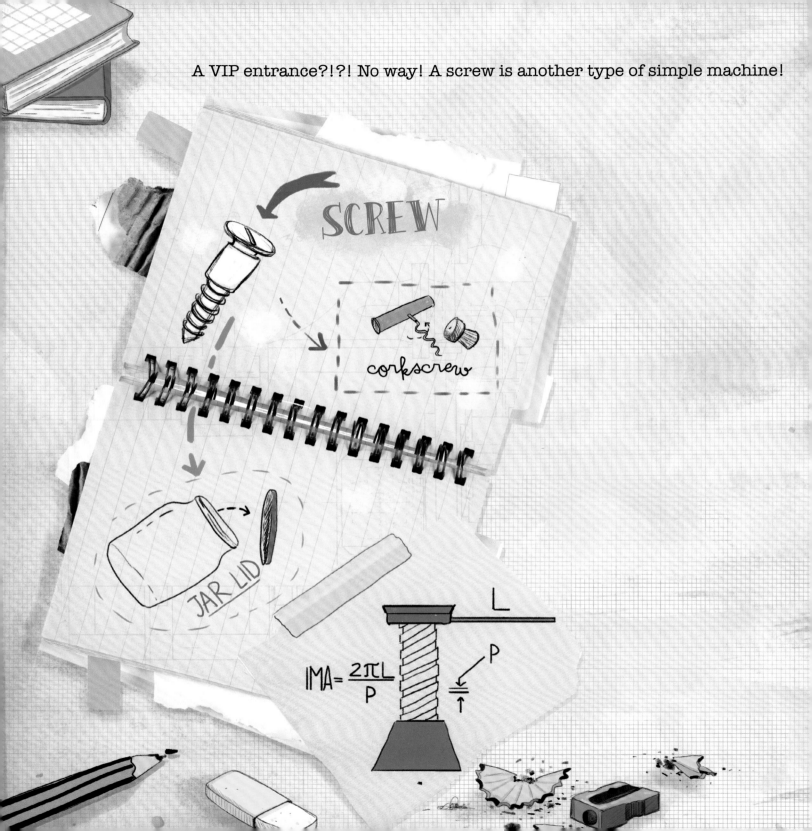

inclined plane

wheel & axle

In fact, a screw is a special kind of inclined plane where the inclined plane (the thread) is wrapped around a pole. As we turn the screw, the incline of the thread slowly makes its way into the wood at a slight angle.

The slight angle of the thread makes the screw go in easier than if you were to try to bang the screw straight in.

How does an ax split wood into pieces?
Does the ax start an argument between the two halves of wood
until they storm away from each other?

An argument?!?! No way! The ax works as a simple machine called a wedge!

WEDGE

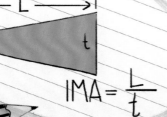

$$IMA = \frac{L}{t}$$

A wedge is made up of two inclined planes put together. It can split wood because the force of an ax meets the wood where the ax is sharpest. The sharp blade can more easily enter the wood than if it were flat.

Then, as the ax moves into the wood the widening ax head pushes the wood outward causing it to separate.

input force

output force

LEVER: a stiff bar that rests on a support called a fulcrum.

Did you know when you play hockey you're using a lever?

BOTTLE OPENER

HOCKEY STICK

STAPLER

WHEEL AND AXLE: a wheel with a rod called an axle through its center.

Did you know a doorknob is a wheel and axle?

wheel

axle

DOORKNOB

input

output

screwdriver

BICYCLE WHEEL

$$IMA = \frac{R}{r}$$

F_e

R

r

F_r

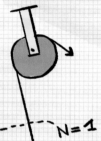

$N = 1$

$F_r \downarrow$

PULLEY: a simple machine that uses grooved wheels and a rope to move a load.

Did you know when a pulley is combined with other pulleys it makes something called a block and tackle?

PULLEY

PULLEY SYSTEM

INCLINED PLANE: a slanting surface connecting a lower level to a higher level.

Did you know stairs are inclined planes?

RAMP

STAIRCASE

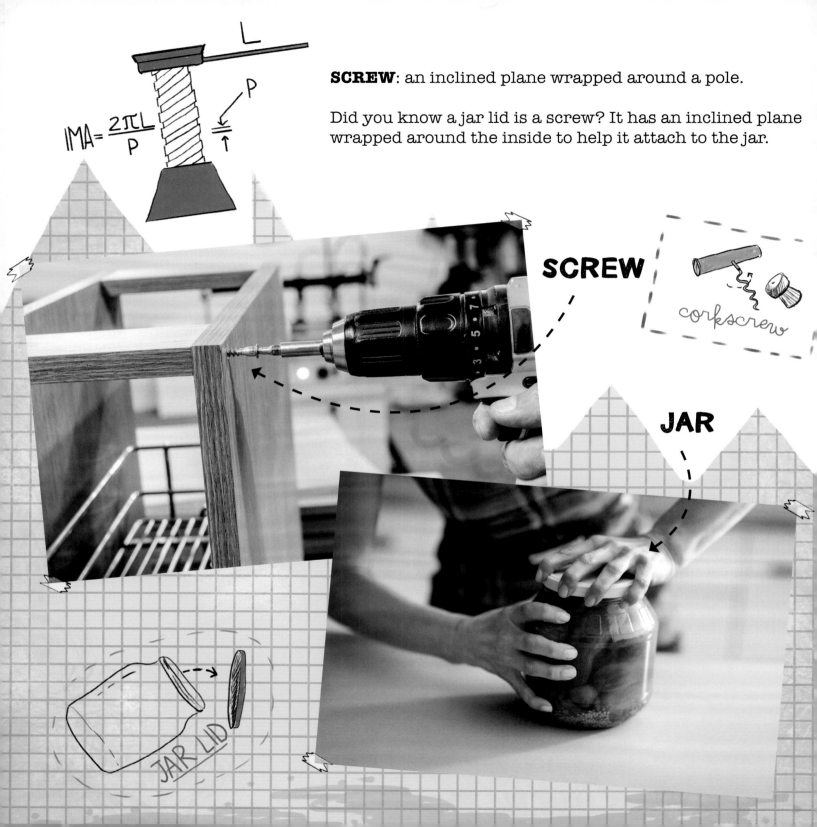

$$IMA = \frac{2\pi L}{P}$$

SCREW: an inclined plane wrapped around a pole.

Did you know a jar lid is a screw? It has an inclined plane wrapped around the inside to help it attach to the jar.

SCREW

corkscrew

JAR

JAR LID

WEDGE: a simple machine made of one inclined plane or two inclined planes put together.

Did you know wedges can be used as doorstops?

DOORSTOP

KNIFE

WEDGE

knife

SCREW

corkscrew